BHARAT VATSA

Digital Nomad LifeStyle

A Guide to Working and Living Anywhere

BharatVatsa

Table of Contents

Title Page
Blank Page
Copyright Page
Author biography
Epigraph
Preface
Introduction
PART 1 - GETTING STARTED
1. Understanding the Digital Nomad Movement
2. Is the Digital Nomad Life Right for you
3. Choosing Your Digital Nomad Career
4. Essential Tools and Technologies
Part 2 - Planning Your Journey
1. Financial Planning and Budgeting
2. Legalities & Logistics
3. Health & Insurance
4. Packing Smart
Part-3: Living the Nomad Life
1. Finding Your Home Base
2. Accommodation Options
3. Staying Productive
4. Building a Community
5. Balancing Work & Leisure
Part-4 - Challenges & Solutions
1. Dealing with Loneliness and Isolation
2. Overcoming Burnout
3. Staying Safe on the Road
Part-5 - Advanced Nomad Strategies
1. Scaling Your Remote Business
2. Passive Income Streams
3. Continuous Learning and Skill Development
CONCLUSION
1. The Future of Digital Nomadism
2. Final Thoughts and Inspiration
Appendices
1. Resources and References
2. Templates and Checklists

DIGITAL NOMAD LIFESTYLE

A GUIDE TO WORKING AND LIVING ANYWHERE

BY

BHARAT VATSA

BharatVatsa

ISBN 12345678901 2345
© Bharat Vatsa 2024

Published in India 2024 by Pencil

A brand of
One Point Six Technologies Pvt. Ltd.
Unit no. 26, Ground Floor, Building A1,
Wadala Truck Terminal Road,
Near Post Office, Antop Hill, Mumbai - 400037
E connect@thepencilapp.com
W www.thepencilapp.com

All rights reserved worldwide

No part of this publication may be reproduced, stored in or introduced into a retrieval system, or transmitted, in any form, or by any means (electronic, mechanical, photocopying, recording, or otherwise), without the prior written permission of the Publisher. Any person who commits an unauthorized act in relation to this publication can be liable to criminal prosecution and civil claims for damages.

DISCLAIMER: The opinions expressed in this book are those of the authors and do not purport to reflect the views of the Publisher.

Author Biography

BharatVatsa

Bharat Vatsa is a seasoned IT Professional with a career spanning over two decades. His expertise and dedication have established him as a trusted leader in the industry.

Born and raised in India, Bharat's journey in the world of technology and management began with his academic pursuits. He holds a Master's degree and many other certifications which laid the foundation for his successful career. Over the years, Bharat has worked with various multinational companies, where he has honed his skills in managing complex projects, optimizing IT services, and driving business efficiencies.

Beyond his professional achievements, Bharat is an avid adventurer with a passion for motorbike journeys. He is a founder of his Riding Club in Pune, INDIA and also admin of Bikers Club Association, PAN India. With over 2 lakh kms in his kitty, he has traversed various terrains, experiencing the thrill and freedom that come with motorbike adventures. This love for exploration is mirrored in his personal and professional life, where he continuously seeks new challenges and opportunities for growth.

Bharat is also a podcast enthusiast and an aspiring DJ. He hosts motivating podcasts on multiple platforms like Spotify, YouTube, Apple Podcast, etc. where he engages with individuals highlighting their achievements and overcoming their challenges through passion. His DJing hobby allows him to express his creativity and connect with people through music, adding another layer to his multifaceted personality.

Poetry & writing blogs/books is yet one of his other passions....

In his book "Digital Nomad Lifestyle", Bharat combines his professional expertise with his personal passions, offering readers a comprehensive guide to navigating the complexities of modern life and work. His practical advice, enriched with personal anecdotes from his motorbike adventures and experiences in the digital space, provides a unique perspective that resonates with readers seeking to balance productivity and passion.

Epigraph

"To move, to breathe, to fly, to float, to gain all while you give, to roam the roads of lands remote, to travel is to live." — Hans Christian Andersen

BharatVatsa

Preface

This book is dedicated to all the Digital Nomads out there in the world... who travel freely while working remotely using technology and the internet. Such people generally have minimal material possessions and work remotely in temporary housing, hotels, cafes, public libraries, co-working spaces, or recreational vehicles, using Wi-Fi, smartphones or mobile hotspots to access the Internet. The majority of digital nomads describe themselves as programmers, content creators, designers, or developers. Some digital nomads are perpetual travellers, while others only maintain the lifestyle for a short period of time. While some nomads travel through multiple countries, others remain in one area, and some may choose to travel while living in a vehicle, in a practice often known as van-dwelling.

My motorbike adventures have taken me across diverse terrains, offering a sense of freedom and excitement that parallels the journey of personal growth. My interest in podcasts has allowed me to engage with thought leaders and experts, broadening my perspectives and inspiring new ideas. And my hobby as a DJ has given me a creative outlet, helping me connect with others through the universal language of music. By weaving together these professional insights and personal stories, I hope to provide you with a holistic approach to navigating the complexities of modern life and work. Whether you are a seasoned professional seeking new strategies for career advancement, a digital nomad looking for practical tips on maintaining productivity and balance, or simply someone interested in personal development, this book offers something for you.

Thank you for joining me on this journey. I hope that the experiences and insights shared in these pages will inspire you to pursue your passions, achieve your goals, and create a life that is both successful and fulfilling.

Happy Reading!
Bharat Vatsa

Digital Nomad Lifestyle

Introduction

1. Welcome to the Digital Nomad Life

The digital nomad lifestyle represents a paradigm shift in how we work and live. It's about breaking free from the traditional 9-to-5 office environment and embracing the freedom to work from anywhere in the world. This book aims to be your comprehensive guide to navigating and thriving in this exciting lifestyle.

2. What is the Digital Nomad Lifestyle?

Digital nomads leverage technology to earn a living while enjoying the flexibility to travel and explore different parts of the world. They often work remotely, either for themselves as freelancers, entrepreneurs, or for companies that offer remote work options. This lifestyle is characterized by a strong desire for adventure, flexibility, and independence.

Key Aspects of the Digital Nomad Lifestyle:
1. Location Independence: The ability to choose your work location, whether it's a bustling city, a serene beach, or a quiet mountain village.
2. Flexibility: Control over your schedule, allowing you to balance work with travel, leisure, and personal growth.

9

3. **Minimalism:** Embracing a minimalist lifestyle by prioritizing experiences over possessions and learning to live with less.
4. **Community:** Connecting with like-minded individuals around the globe, forming a supportive network of fellow nomads.
5. **Continuous Learning:** Adapting to new cultures, languages, and ways of life while constantly upgrading your skills to stay competitive in the remote work market.

What Readers Can Expect from This Book:

This book is designed to be a practical and inspirational guide for anyone interested in the digital nomad lifestyle, whether you are a seasoned traveler or just starting out. Here's what you can expect:

1. **Comprehensive Information:** In-depth insights into the digital nomad lifestyle, including its benefits and challenges.
2. **Step-by-Step Guidance:** Clear, actionable steps to transition from a traditional work setup to a location-independent career.
3. **Practical Tips and Advice:** Expert advice on managing finances, staying productive, finding accommodation, and dealing with legal and logistical issues.
4. **Personal Stories and Case Studies:** Real-life examples of successful digital nomads who share their experiences, tips, and lessons learned.
5. **Resource Lists:** Curated lists of tools, apps, websites, and communities to help you navigate your digital nomad journey.
6. **Inspiration and Motivation:** Encouragement and motivational insights to help you overcome challenges and stay committed to your goals.

By the end of this book, you will have a thorough understanding of what it takes to live and work as a digital nomad. You'll be equipped with the knowledge, tools, and confidence to embark on your own adventure, exploring new places while maintaining a successful and fulfilling career. Welcome to the exciting world of digital nomadism!

PART1 - GETTING STARTED

1. Understanding the Digital Nomad Movement

History and evolution of the digital nomad lifestyle

Early Beginnings
The digital nomad lifestyle, as we know it today, has its roots in several historical and technological developments that date back decades. The concept of working remotely is not entirely new; it can be traced back to the late 20th century when advancements in communication technology began to change the nature of work

1. Telecommuting in the 1970s and 1980s: The term "telecommuting" was coined in the 1970s as businesses started experimenting with allowing employees to work from home. This was primarily driven by the oil crisis, which made commuting more expensive and less practical. Early telecommuters used landline telephones and rudimentary computer networks to perform their duties.
2. Rise of Personal Computing in the 1980s and 1990s: The advent of personal computers and the development of the internet in the 1980s and 1990s laid the groundwork for remote work. As computers became more affordable and internet connections more widespread, the possibility of working from anywhere became increasingly feasible.

Digital Nomad Lifestyle

The Internet Boom and Early Remote Work
1. **The Dot-Com Boom (Late 1990s to Early 2000s):** The dot-com boom brought a significant shift in how businesses operated, with many tech companies and startups adopting more flexible work policies. This period saw the rise of freelance work and the gig economy, facilitated by online platforms like Elance (now Upwork) and Freelancer.com.
2. **Early Digital Nomads:** During this time, a few pioneers began to experiment with the idea of combining work and travel. Equipped with laptops and mobile phones, these early digital nomads took advantage of their newfound mobility to explore the world while maintaining their professional careers.

The 2000s: A Growing Movement
1. **Wi-Fi and Mobile Technology:** The widespread availability of Wi-Fi in cafes, airports, and public spaces, along with the proliferation of mobile technology, significantly boosted the digital nomad movement. Smartphones and portable Wi-Fi devices allowed for constant connectivity, making it easier for individuals to work from virtually anywhere.
2. **Remote Work Acceptance:** By the mid-2000s, remote work had gained more acceptance among employers. Companies like Basecamp (formerly 37signals) and Automattic (the company behind WordPress) championed remote work, proving that businesses could thrive without a centralized office.

The 2010s: Mainstream Adoption
1. **Co-Working Spaces:** The rise of co-working spaces in the early 2010s provided digital nomads with a sense of community and a professional work environment. Spaces like WeWork and Regus became popular among remote workers, offering flexible memberships and networking opportunities.
2. **Digital Nomad Communities:** Online communities and forums dedicated to digital nomads began to flourish. Websites like Nomad List and forums such as Reddit's r/digital nomad provided valuable resources, destination guides, and a platform for sharing experiences and advice.
3. **Influencers and Bloggers:** Influencers, bloggers, and authors who embraced the digital nomad lifestyle started to gain prominence. Books like "The 4-Hour Workweek" by Tim Ferriss inspired many to seek alternative ways of working and living, promoting the idea that one could achieve financial independence and location freedom.

The Impact of COVID-19
1. **Pandemic-Driven Remote Work:** The COVID-19 pandemic in 2020 had a profound impact on the digital nomad movement. With lockdowns and social distancing measures in place, millions of people were forced to work from home. This accelerated the adoption of remote work practices and demonstrated to both employers and employees that remote work was not only possible but often preferable.
2. **Surge in Digital Nomadism:** As restrictions eased, many who had experienced remote work for the first time chose to continue working remotely, opting for a more nomadic lifestyle. Countries began to recognize the potential economic benefits of attracting digital nomads and started offering specialized visas and incentives to encourage longer stays.

13

The Birth of a Movement

The digital nomad movement is a modern phenomenon that combines the freedom of travel with the ability to work remotely, thanks to advancements in technology. The term "digital nomad" describes individuals who utilize telecommunications technologies to earn a living and conduct their life in a nomadic manner. These individuals often work remotely from foreign countries, coffee shops, public libraries, co-working spaces, or recreational vehicles.

Technological Advancements

The digital nomad lifestyle wouldn't be possible without key technological advancements:
1. Internet Access: The global proliferation of high-speed internet has been the most crucial factor. With reliable internet connections available in even remote parts of the world, digital nomads can stay connected and work from virtually anywhere.
2. Cloud Computing: Tools like Google Drive, Dropbox, and other cloud-based services allow for seamless file sharing and collaboration across borders.
3. Communication Platforms: Applications like Slack, Zoom, and Skype enable real-time communication, making it easy to stay in touch with colleagues and clients regardless of location.
4. Project Management Tools: Platforms such as Trello, Asana, and Basecamp facilitate project coordination and task management, ensuring that remote teams remain productive and organized.

The Appeal of the Digital Nomad Lifestyle

Several factors contribute to the growing appeal of the digital nomad lifestyle:

1. Freedom and Flexibility: The ability to choose where and when to work is incredibly appealing. Digital nomads can structure their days to suit their personal preferences and peak productivity times.
2. Travel and Exploration: The opportunity to explore new cultures, languages, and environments while working is a significant draw. Digital nomads often choose destinations based on personal interests, affordability, and lifestyle preferences.
3. Cost of Living: Many digital nomads take advantage of the lower cost of living in various countries. This financial flexibility allows them to save more, invest in experiences, or build their businesses.
4. Work-Life Balance: The ability to design a work-life balance that aligns with individual goals and values is a significant motivator. This lifestyle often leads to increased job satisfaction and overall well-being.

Challenges of the Digital Nomad Lifestyle

While the digital nomad lifestyle offers numerous benefits, it also comes with its own set of challenges:

1. Loneliness and Isolation: Constant travel can lead to feelings of isolation and loneliness. Building and maintaining relationships can be difficult when frequently changing locations.
2. Work-Life Boundaries: Without a traditional office setting, it can be challenging to establish clear boundaries between work and personal life.

3. Legal and Financial Issues: Navigating visas, work permits, and taxation can be complex. Digital nomads need to be aware of the legal requirements of the countries they visit.
4. Health and Safety: Access to healthcare, maintaining a healthy lifestyle, and staying safe in unfamiliar places are important considerations.

The Future of the Digital Nomad Movement

The digital nomad movement shows no signs of slowing down. As remote work becomes increasingly accepted and supported by employers, more people are likely to embrace this lifestyle. Additionally, the rise of co-living and co-working spaces specifically designed for digital nomads provides a supportive infrastructure that fosters community and collaboration.

Governments and cities are also recognizing the potential economic benefits of attracting digital nomads. Some countries have started offering digital nomad visas to encourage longer stays and economic contributions from these travelers.

In conclusion, the digital nomad movement is a testament to the evolving nature of work in the 21st century. It represents a shift towards greater flexibility, autonomy, and the blending of work and travel. As technology continues to advance, the possibilities for living and working as a digital nomad will only expand, offering new opportunities and challenges for those who choose this path. It has come a long way from its early beginnings in telecommuting. It has evolved into a global movement that offers unprecedented freedom and flexibility. As technology continues to advance and work cultures adapt, the digital nomad lifestyle is poised to become an integral part of the future of work.

2. Is the Digital Nomad Life Right for you

Self-assessment and considerations for aspiring digital nomads

Becoming a digital nomad is an exciting prospect, but it's essential to assess whether this lifestyle aligns with your personal and professional goals. Here are key self-assessment questions and considerations to help you determine if the digital nomad life is right for you:

Self-Assessment Questions

1. Why Do You Want to Become a Digital Nomad? Identify your primary motivations. Are you seeking adventure, flexibility, work-life balance, or the opportunity to explore new cultures? Understanding your reasons will help you stay focused and committed.

2. Are You Comfortable with Uncertainty? The digital nomad lifestyle often involves unpredictability, such as fluctuating income, changing environments, and occasional travel disruptions. Assess your tolerance for uncertainty and your ability to adapt to new situations.

3. Do You Have Strong Time Management Skills? Remote work requires self-discipline and excellent time management. Evaluate your ability to set and stick to a schedule, meet deadlines, and manage your workload independently.

Digital Nomad Lifestyle

4. Can You Work Independently? Digital nomads often work alone or with minimal supervision. Consider whether you are self-motivated and capable of working without the structure of a traditional office environment.
5. Are You Tech-Savvy? Comfort with technology is crucial for digital nomads. Ensure you are proficient with the tools and platforms necessary for remote work, such as communication apps, project management software, and cybersecurity measures.
6. How Do You Handle Loneliness and Isolation? Traveling and working alone can lead to feelings of loneliness. Reflect on your social needs and whether you can find ways to connect with others while on the move.
7. Are You Financially Prepared? Assess your financial situation, including savings, income stability, and budgeting skills. Being financially prepared can help you navigate the ups and downs of a nomadic lifestyle.
8. Do You Have a Support System? Consider whether you have friends, family, or a community you can rely on for support, both emotionally and practically, as you transition to a digital nomad lifestyle.

Practical Considerations

1. Job and Income Stability: Evaluate whether your current job or business can be done remotely. If you are a freelancer or entrepreneur, ensure you have a stable client base or business model that supports remote work.
2. Legal and Visa Requirements: Research visa and work permit requirements for the countries you plan to visit. Some countries offer digital nomad visas that allow extended stays for remote workers.
3. Health and Insurance: Plan for healthcare needs and secure appropriate travel and health insurance. Consider how you will access medical care while traveling.
4. Communication: Ensure you have reliable internet access and communication tools to stay connected with clients, colleagues, and loved ones. Consider investing in backup internet solutions, such as mobile hotspots.
5. Accommodation and Cost of Living: Research the cost of living in potential destinations and explore accommodation options, such as co-living spaces, short-term rentals, and hostels. Plan your budget accordingly.
6. Work Environment: Think about your ideal work environment. Will you be productive in cafes, co-working spaces, or your accommodation? Ensure you can create a conducive work environment wherever you go.
7. Cultural Adaptation: Prepare for cultural differences and language barriers. Learn basic phrases in the local language and familiarize yourself with cultural norms to make your stay more enjoyable.

Creating a Transition Plan

1. Start Small: Consider taking a short-term trip to test the digital nomad lifestyle before committing long-term. This will help you understand the challenges and rewards of working remotely while traveling.
2. Set Clear Goals: Define your personal and professional goals for becoming a digital nomad. Establish a timeline and actionable steps to achieve these goals.

3. **Build a Support Network:** Connect with other digital nomads through online communities, social media, and networking events. Building a support network can provide valuable advice, encouragement, and companionship.
4. **Develop a Routine:** Create a daily routine that balances work, travel, and leisure. Having a routine can help you stay productive and maintain a sense of normalcy.
5. **Stay Flexible:** Be prepared to adapt your plans as needed. Flexibility is key to successfully navigating the challenges and opportunities of the digital nomad lifestyle.

By conducting a thorough self-assessment and considering the practical aspects of the digital nomad lifestyle, you can make an informed decision about whether this path is right for you. If you decide to pursue it, these steps will help you transition smoothly and set yourself up for success.

3. Choosing Your Digital Nomad Career

Types of remote jobs and freelance opportunities suitable for digital nomads

The digital nomad lifestyle offers a wide range of remote jobs and freelance opportunities that can be performed from anywhere with an internet connection. Here are some of the most popular and viable options:

Remote Jobs

1. Software Development and Programming: Roles: Web Developer, Mobile App Developer, Software Engineer, Front-End Developer, Back-End Developer, Full Stack Developer. Skills Required: Proficiency in programming languages such as JavaScript, Python, Java, C#, Ruby, and experience with frameworks and libraries

2. Graphic and Web Design: Roles: Graphic Designer, UX/UI Designer, Web Designer, Illustrator. Skills Required: Proficiency in design software such as Adobe Creative Suite (Photoshop, Illustrator, InDesign), Sketch, Figma, and knowledge of HTML/CSS.

3. Content Creation and Writing: Roles: Content Writer, Copywriter, Blogger, Technical Writer, Editor, Proofreader. Skills Required: Strong writing and editing skills, knowledge of SEO, and proficiency in content management systems (CMS) like WordPress.

BharatVatsa

4. **Digital Marketing:** Roles: Social Media Manager, SEO Specialist, PPC Specialist, Email Marketing Specialist, Content Marketing Manager. Skills Required: Understanding of digital marketing strategies, proficiency in marketing tools (Google Analytics, SEMrush, HubSpot), and experience with social media platforms.
5. **Customer Support and Service:** Roles: Customer Support Representative, Technical Support Specialist, Customer Success Manager. Skills Required: Strong communication skills, problem-solving abilities, and experience with customer support software (Zendesk, Freshdesk).
6. **Virtual Assistance:** Roles: Virtual Assistant, Executive Assistant, Administrative Assistant. Skills Required: Organizational and multitasking skills, proficiency in office software (Microsoft Office, Google Workspace), and experience with project management tools (Trello, Asana).
7. **Sales and Business Development:** Roles: Sales Representative, Business Development Manager, Account Manager. Skills Required: Strong communication and negotiation skills, experience with CRM software (Salesforce, HubSpot CRM).
8. **Online Teaching and Tutoring:** Roles: ESL Teacher, Subject Tutor, Online Course Instructor. Skills Required: Teaching or tutoring experience, proficiency in video conferencing tools (Zoom, Skype), and knowledge of the subject matter.

Freelance Opportunities

1. **Freelance Writing and Blogging:** Projects: Articles, blog posts, e-books, copywriting, technical writing. Platforms: Upwork, Freelancer, ProBlogger, Contena.
2. **Freelance Graphic Design:** Projects: Logos, branding, marketing materials, illustrations, web design. Platforms: 99designs, Dribbble, Behance, Fiverr.
3. **Freelance Web Development:** Projects: Website development, web applications, e-commerce sites, website maintenance. Platforms: Upwork, Freelancer, Toptal, Codeable.
4. **Freelance Digital Marketing:** Projects: SEO optimization, social media campaigns, PPC advertising, content marketing. Platforms: Upwork, Freelancer, Fiverr, PeoplePerHour.
5. **Freelance Video Editing and Animation:** Projects: Video editing, motion graphics, animations, explainer videos. Platforms: Upwork, Freelancer, Fiverr, VideoHive.
6. **Freelance Photography:** Projects: Stock photography, event photography, product photography, photo editing. Platforms: Shutterstock, Adobe Stock, Alamy, 500px.
7. **Freelance Consulting:** Projects: Business strategy, financial consulting, marketing consulting, HR consulting. Platforms: Clarity.fm, Upwork, Freelancer, Catalant.
8. **Freelance Translation and Interpretation:** Projects: Document translation, website localization, interpretation services. Platforms: Upwork, ProZ, Gengo, OneHourTranslation.

Emerging Remote Opportunities

1. **Remote Project Management:** Roles: Project Manager, Scrum Master, Agile Coach. Skills Required: Project management certifications (PMP, ScrumMaster), experience with project management tools (Jira, Monday.com).

2. **Remote Healthcare and Telemedicine:** Roles: Telehealth Doctor, Remote Nurse, Mental Health Counselor. Skills Required: Relevant medical or counseling qualifications, proficiency in telemedicine platforms.

3. **Remote Legal Services:** Roles: Remote Lawyer, Paralegal, Legal Consultant. Skills Required: Legal qualifications, knowledge of relevant legal systems, experience with legal research tools.

Tips for Finding Remote Work and Freelance Opportunities

1. **Build a Strong Online Presence:** Create a professional website or portfolio showcasing your skills, experience, and previous work. Use LinkedIn to network and connect with potential clients or employers.
2. **Leverage Job Boards and Freelance Platforms:** Regularly check remote job boards (We Work Remotely, Remote.co, FlexJobs) and freelance platforms (Upwork, Freelancer, Fiverr) for opportunities that match your skills.
3. **Network with Other Digital Nomads:** Join online communities and forums where digital nomads share job leads, tips, and advice. Attend virtual or in-person events to expand your network.
4. **Develop In-Demand Skills:** Continuously update your skills and stay informed about industry trends. Consider taking online courses or obtaining certifications in areas with high demand.
5. **Tailor Your Applications:** Customize your resumes and cover letters for each job application. Highlight relevant skills and experience that align with the specific requirements of the job.

By exploring these remote job and freelance opportunities, aspiring digital nomads can find the right fit for their skills and lifestyle preferences, paving the way for a successful and fulfilling career on the road.

4. Essential Tools and Technologies

Must-have gadgets, software, and apps for productivity and connectivity
Gadgets

1. Laptop: Example: MacBook Pro, Dell XPS, Lenovo ThinkPad. Features: Lightweight, durable, long battery life, powerful performance.
2. Smartphone: Example: iPhone, Samsung Galaxy, Google Pixel. Features: High-quality camera, long battery life, large storage capacity.
3. Portable Wi-Fi Hotspot: Example: Skyroam Solis, GlocalMe G4 Pro, NETGEAR Nighthawk M1. Features: Global coverage, fast internet speeds, long battery life.
4. Noise-Cancelling Headphones: Example: Bose QuietComfort 35, Sony WH-1000XM4, Apple AirPods Pro. Features: Excellent noise cancellation, long battery life, comfortable fit.
5. External Hard Drive/SSD: Example: Samsung T5 SSD, Seagate Backup Plus, Western Digital My Passport. Features: High storage capacity, fast data transfer speeds, compact design.
6. Portable Charger/Power Bank: Example: Anker PowerCore, RAVPower, Mophie Powerstation. Features: High capacity, fast charging, multiple ports.
Universal Travel Adapter: Example: Epicka Universal Travel Adapter, Bestek Travel Power Converter. Features: Compatibility with multiple plug types, USB ports, surge protection.
7. Portable Monitor: Example: ASUS ZenScreen, AOC e1659Fwu, HP EliteDisplay. Features: Lightweight, USB-powered, high resolution.

Digital Nomad Lifestyle

8. Bluetooth Keyboard and Mouse: Example: Logitech K380, Apple Magic Keyboard, Microsoft Surface Arc Mouse. Features: Compact, ergonomic, long battery life.
9. Cable Organizer: Example: BAGSMART Electronics Organizer, ProCase Travel Gear Organizer. Features: Multiple compartments, durable material, compact design.

Software and Apps

1. Communication: Slack: Team communication and collaboration. Zoom: Video conferencing and virtual meetings. Skype: Video and voice calls, messaging. etc.
2. Project Management: Trello: Task management and collaboration. Asana: Project tracking and team management.Monday.com: Workflow and project management etc.
3. Cloud Storage: Google Drive: Cloud storage and file sharing. Dropbox: File storage and synchronization. OneDrive: Microsoft cloud storage solution.
4. Productivity: Notion: All-in-one workspace for notes, tasks, and collaboration. Evernote: Note-taking and organization. Todoist: Task management and to-do lists. etc.
5. Time Management: RescueTime: Time tracking and productivity analysis. Toggl: Time tracking for tasks and projects. Clockify: Time tracking and timesheet management.
6. Finance Management: Mint: Budgeting and expense tracking. YNAB (You Need a Budget): Budgeting and financial planning. Expensify: Expense reporting and receipt tracking.
7. VPN Service: ExpressVPN: Secure and fast VPN service. NordVPN: Privacy-focused VPN with global servers. CyberGhost: User-friendly VPN with strong encryption.
8. Travel and Accommodation: Airbnb: Accommodation booking platform.Booking.com: Hotel and accommodation booking. Nomad List: Community and resources for digital nomads. etc.
9. Language Learning: Duolingo: Language learning app. Babbel: Interactive language courses. Memrise: Language learning with real-life content.
10. Security: LastPass: Password manager. 1Password: Password manager and secure storage. Bitdefender: Antivirus and cybersecurity software.
11. File Management: WinRAR/7-Zip: File compression and extraction. FileZilla: FTP client for file transfers. Microsoft Office 365: Office suite for productivity.

Apps for Connectivity and Lifestyle

1. Travel Planning: TripIt: Travel itinerary and planning. Hopper: Flight and hotel booking with price predictions. Skyscanner: Flight, hotel, and car rental search. etc.
2. Local Connectivity: Meetup: Connecting with local groups and events. Couchsurfing: Connecting with locals for free accommodation. Eventbrite: Finding local events and activities.
3. Health and Fitness: MyFitnessPal: Nutrition and fitness tracking. Headspace: Meditation and mindfulness. Strava: Running and cycling tracking. etc.
4. Language Translation: Google Translate: Instant language translation. iTranslate: Translation and dictionary. Microsoft Translator: Text and voice translation.

By equipping yourself with these essential gadgets, software, and apps, you can enhance your productivity and connectivity as a digital nomad. These tools will help you stay organized, maintain strong communication, and navigate the challenges of working remotely from various locations around the world.

PART:2 - PLANNING YOUR JOURNEY

1. Financial Planning and Budgeting

Managing finances, saving, and budgeting for a sustainable nomadic lifestyle

Adopting a digital nomad lifestyle can offer unparalleled freedom, but it requires careful financial planning and management to ensure sustainability. Here's a guide to help you manage your finances, save effectively, and budget wisely:

1. Assessing and Planning Your Finances
   - Calculate Your Monthly Expenses: Accommodation: Rent, utilities, maintenance. Food and Groceries: Eating out, groceries, delivery services. Transportation: Flights, local travel, fuel, car rentals. Insurance: Health, travel, property. Communication: Phone bills, internet. Work Expenses: Co-working spaces, software subscriptions, equipment. Miscellaneous: Entertainment, clothing, healthcare.
   - Estimate Your Income: Assess your expected income from remote work or freelance gigs. Consider any passive income sources like investments, rental income, or royalties.
   - Create a Budget: Use a budgeting tool or app (e.g., Mint, YNAB) to track your income and expenses. Set spending limits for each category based on your income and savings goals. Allocate a portion of your income to an emergency fund.

Digital Nomad Lifestyle

- Emergency Fund: Save at least 3-6 months' worth of living expenses to cover unexpected costs or income gaps.

2. Saving and Investment Strategies
- Automate Savings: Set up automatic transfers to your savings account to ensure regular contributions.
- High-Interest Savings Accounts: Use high-yield savings accounts or money market accounts to earn better interest rates on your savings.
- Invest Wisely: Diversify your investments across stocks, bonds, mutual funds, or ETFs to grow your wealth. Consider using robo-advisors or financial planners for investment guidance.
- Retirement Planning: Contribute regularly to retirement accounts (e.g., IRAs, 401(k)s). If self-employed, consider SEP IRAs or Solo 401(k)s for higher contribution limits.

3. Budgeting for a Nomadic Lifestyle
- Research Cost of Living: Use resources like Numbeo, Nomad List, or Expatistan to compare the cost of living in different destinations. Choose locations that align with your budget and financial goals.
- Accommodation Strategies: Use platforms like Airbnb, Booking.com, or local rental sites for short-term stays. Consider house-sitting or home exchanges to save on accommodation costs. Negotiate for long-term rental discounts.
- Travel Hacks: Use flight comparison sites (e.g., Skyscanner, Google Flights) to find the best deals. Take advantage of travel reward programs and credit card points. Travel during off-peak times to save on airfares and accommodation.
- Meal Planning: Cook meals at home to save on dining expenses. Explore local markets for affordable and fresh produce. Set a budget for dining out and stick to it.
- Work Expenses: Opt for co-working spaces with flexible membership plans. Utilize free or affordable software alternatives for your work needs. Invest in durable and multi-functional equipment to minimize replacement costs.

4. Managing Currency and Payments
- Multi-Currency Accounts: Use banks or services that offer multi-currency accounts to reduce currency exchange fees. TransferWise (now Wise) and Revolut are popular options for digital nomads.
- Credit and Debit Cards: Choose cards with low or no foreign transaction fees. Look for travel rewards cards that offer points or cashback on travel-related expenses.
- Payment Platforms: Use platforms like PayPal, Stripe, or Payoneer for easy international transactions. Consider using cryptocurrencies for secure and low-cost transfers.
- Track Exchange Rates: Use apps like XE or OANDA to monitor exchange rates and convert money when rates are favorable.

27

5. **Regular Financial Review**
   - **Monthly Review:** Review your budget and spending at the end of each month. Adjust your budget categories based on your spending patterns and financial goals.
   - **Quarterly Review:** Assess your savings and investment progress every quarter. Make necessary adjustments to your savings rate or investment strategy.
   - **Annual Review:** Evaluate your overall financial health and set new financial goals for the year. Review your insurance coverage and make updates if needed.

6. **Tips for Staying Financially Disciplined**
   - **Set Financial Goals:** Define short-term and long-term financial goals to stay motivated. Track your progress towards these goals regularly.
   - **Avoid Debt:** Minimize the use of credit cards unless you can pay off the balance in full each month. Avoid taking loans unless absolutely necessary.
   - **Stay Informed:** Educate yourself about personal finance and investment strategies. Follow financial blogs, podcasts, or take online courses to enhance your knowledge.

By implementing these strategies and tools, you can manage your finances effectively, save diligently, and budget wisely, ensuring a sustainable and enjoyable digital nomad lifestyle.

Digital Nomad Lifestyle

2. Legalities & Logistics

Visas, work permits, and understanding tax implications
Embarking on a digital nomad lifestyle requires careful planning and understanding of visa requirements, work permits, and tax implications in various countries. Here's a guide to help you navigate these aspects:

1. Research Visa Requirements
- Understand Visa Types: Research the types of visas available in your desired destinations (e.g., tourist, business, digital nomad visas). Check the duration of stay allowed and any restrictions on work activities.
- Check Visa Requirements: Visit the official government websites or consult with embassies/consulates of the countries you plan to visit. Note the application process, required documents, and fees.
- Apply for Long-Term Visas: For extended stays, consider applying for long-term visas or digital nomad visas if available. Some countries offer specific visas for remote workers, providing legal status to work while traveling.

2. Obtain Work Permits (if Necessary)
- Check Work Permit Requirements: Determine if you need a work permit based on your activities (e.g., freelance work, remote employment). Some countries allow remote work without a specific work permit, but regulations vary.

29

- Apply for Work Permits: Follow the application process outlined by the relevant authorities. Provide necessary documents such as proof of employment, financial stability, and health insurance.
- Consult with Legal Experts: Consider seeking advice from immigration lawyers or consultants familiar with the visa and work permit requirements in your chosen destinations.

3. Understand Tax Implications
- Tax Residency: Understand the concept of tax residency and how it applies to digital nomads. Tax residency rules vary by country and can depend on the duration of stay and other factors.
- Tax Planning: Research tax treaties between your home country and the countries you plan to visit. Consider structuring your income to minimize tax liabilities, such as using tax-efficient investment accounts.
- Consult with Tax Professionals: Seek advice from tax professionals who specialize in international taxation for guidance on your specific situation. Ensure compliance with tax laws in both your home country and the countries you visit.
- Keep Detailed Records: Maintain accurate records of your income, expenses, and travel dates. This information may be required for tax filings and to prove your tax residency status.

4. Additional Tips
- Travel Insurance: Purchase comprehensive travel insurance that includes medical coverage and emergency evacuation. Consider insurance policies that cover remote work-related issues, such as equipment theft or loss.
- Healthcare: Research healthcare options in your destinations, including access to medical facilities and health insurance requirements. Carry necessary medications and copies of medical records.
- Digital Security: Use secure internet connections and consider using a virtual private network (VPN) for online security. Keep backups of important documents and data in secure cloud storage.
- Community and Resources: Join digital nomad communities and forums to connect with others and share experiences. Stay informed about visa, work permit, and tax updates through online resources and newsletters.

By carefully planning your visa, work permit, and tax obligations, you can enjoy a sustainable digital nomad lifestyle while complying with legal requirements in your chosen destinations.

3. Health & Insurance

Staying healthy on the road and securing the right insurance coverage

Maintaining good health and having the right insurance coverage are essential aspects of a sustainable digital nomad lifestyle. Here's a guide to help you stay healthy and secure while traveling:

1. Prioritize Health and Wellness
- Regular Exercise: Incorporate physical activity into your routine, such as walking, yoga, or bodyweight exercises. Use fitness apps or online workouts to stay active.
- Healthy Eating: Choose nutritious foods and local produce to maintain a balanced diet. Be mindful of portion sizes and avoid excessive indulgence in unhealthy foods.
- Stay Hydrated: Drink plenty of water, especially in hot or dry climates. Limit consumption of sugary drinks and alcohol.
- Get Adequate Sleep: Aim for 7-9 hours of quality sleep each night. Maintain a consistent sleep schedule, even while traveling.
- Manage Stress: Practice stress-relieving activities such as meditation, mindfulness, or journaling. Engage in hobbies or activities that bring you joy and relaxation.

2. Secure the Right Insurance Coverage

- **Health Insurance:** Obtain international health insurance that covers medical expenses, emergency evacuation, and repatriation. Ensure the policy includes coverage for pre-existing conditions if applicable.
- **Travel Insurance:** Purchase travel insurance that covers trip cancellations, delays, and lost or stolen belongings. Look for policies that include coverage for adventure activities or sports you may participate in.
- **Digital Nomad Insurance:** Consider specialized insurance for digital nomads that includes coverage for equipment, liability, and legal expenses related to remote work. Review the policy carefully to understand the coverage limits and exclusions.
- **Emergency Medical Evacuation Insurance:** Inquire about coverage for emergency medical evacuation to a suitable medical facility in case of serious illness or injury. Ensure the policy covers evacuation to your home country if needed.
- **Additional Coverage:** Depending on your activities and destinations, consider additional coverage for specific needs, such as adventure sports, natural disasters, or political evacuation.

3. Other Health and Safety Tips

- **Stay Informed:** Research health risks and vaccination requirements for your destinations. Stay updated on travel advisories and local health guidelines.
- **Practice Safe Travel:** Use reputable transportation services and follow safety guidelines. Be cautious of your surroundings and avoid risky situations.
- **Seek Medical Advice:** Consult with a healthcare provider before traveling, especially for long-term stays or to remote areas. Carry a first-aid kit and any necessary medications with you.
- **Stay Connected:** Share your travel itinerary with family or friends. Keep important contacts, including emergency services and embassy/consulate information, handy.

By prioritizing your health and securing the right insurance coverage, you can enjoy a safe and fulfilling digital nomad lifestyle, exploring the world while maintaining your well-being.

Digital Nomad Lifestyle

4. Packing Smart

Packing essentials and tips for minimalistic travel

Embracing a minimalistic approach to packing can enhance your travel experience, making it more efficient, enjoyable, and sustainable. Here's a guide to help you pack light and smart for your adventures:

1. Essential Clothing
- **Versatile Clothing:** Pack items that can be mixed and matched to create different outfits. Choose lightweight, quick-drying fabrics that are suitable for various climates.
- **Layering Pieces:** Include a few layers, such as a lightweight jacket, sweater, or scarf, for warmth and versatility.
- **Comfortable Shoes:** Bring a pair of comfortable walking shoes suitable for exploring. Consider collapsible or minimalist footwear to save space.
- **Swimwear and Active Wear:** Pack swimwear and active wear if you plan to engage in water activities or exercise.
- **Weather-Appropriate Gear:** Check the weather forecast and pack accordingly, including rain gear or sun protection.

33

2. Essential Accessories
- **Travel-Sized Toiletries:** Use travel-sized containers for toiletries to save space. Consider solid toiletries, such as shampoo bars, to reduce liquid items.
- **Travel Towel:** Pack a lightweight, quick-drying travel towel for convenience.
- **Travel-Friendly Tech:** Bring essential tech items, such as a smartphone, charger, and adapters. Consider a lightweight laptop or tablet if necessary for work or entertainment.
- **Reusable Water Bottle:** Carry a reusable water bottle to stay hydrated and reduce plastic waste.
- **Daypack or Bag:** Bring a small daypack or bag for daily excursions and to carry essentials.

3. Packing Tips
- **Rolling vs. Folding:** Roll clothes to save space and minimize wrinkles. Use packing cubes or compression bags to organize and compress items.
- **Limit Shoes:** Pack only the shoes you need and wear the bulkiest pair while traveling. Consider shoes that can be dressed up or down for versatility.
- **Multipurpose Items:** Choose items that serve multiple purposes, such as a sarong that can be used as a scarf, towel, or beach cover-up.
- **Minimalist Toiletries:** Simplify your toiletry kit to essentials only. Use solid or multi-use products to reduce the number of items.
- **Laundry Options:** Plan for laundry during your trip to re-wear clothes and pack less. Use laundry services or wash clothes in a sink if facilities are available.

4. Mindful Packing
- **Consider Your Activities:** Pack based on the activities you plan to do and the local culture. Research dress codes and customs to pack appropriately.
- **Leave Room for Souvenirs:** Pack with some extra space for souvenirs or items you may acquire during your travels.
- **Review and Edit:** Before finalizing your packing, review your items and remove anything unnecessary. Be mindful of items you may be able to purchase or borrow at your destination.
- **Stay Organized:** Use packing lists and stay organized to avoid overpacking or forgetting essentials.
- **Practice Minimalism:** Embrace the concept of minimalism in your travels by focusing on experiences rather than possessions. Enjoy the freedom and flexibility of traveling light.

PART-3: LIVING THE NOMAD LIFE

1. Finding Your Home Base

Choosing the best cities and countries for digital nomads

Selecting the right cities and countries as a digital nomad can greatly impact your work-life balance, cost of living, access to amenities, and overall experience. Here are some factors to consider when choosing your next destination:

1. Cost of Living
- Affordability: Look for destinations with a low cost of living to stretch your budget.
- Value for Money: Consider the quality of life and amenities you can afford within your budget.
- Currency Exchange Rate: Check the exchange rate to maximize your purchasing power.

2. Internet Connectivity
- Reliable Internet: Choose cities with reliable and high-speed internet access.
- Co-working Spaces: Look for destinations with co-working spaces or cafes with good internet connectivity.

Digital Nomad Lifestyle

3. **Quality of Life**
   - Safety: Research the safety and security of the destination, especially for solo travelers.
   - Healthcare: Access to quality healthcare facilities and services.
   - Climate: Consider the climate and weather patterns, especially if you have preferences or health considerations.

4. **Digital Nomad Community**
   - Community Support: Choose destinations with an active digital nomad community for networking and support.
   - Events and Meetups: Look for cities with regular events, meetups, and co-working spaces for digital nomads.

5. **Visa and Immigration Policies**
   - Visa Requirements: Check the visa requirements and length of stay allowed for your nationality.
   - Ease of Visa Extension: Consider destinations where it's easy to extend your stay if you decide to stay longer.

6. **Travel Opportunities**
   - Proximity to Other Destinations: Choose a location that allows easy travel to nearby cities or countries for weekend getaways.
   - Transportation: Consider the availability and cost of transportation within the city and to other destinations.

7. **Cultural Experience**
   - Local Culture: Immerse yourself in a new culture with unique traditions, cuisine, and lifestyle.
   - Language: Consider destinations where you can learn or practice a new language.

8. **Time Zone**
   - Work Compatibility: Choose a location with a time zone that aligns with your work schedule or clients' time zones.
   - Remote Work-Friendly: Look for destinations with a culture and infrastructure that support remote work.

9. **Personal Preferences**
   - Urban vs. Rural: Decide if you prefer the hustle and bustle of a city or the tranquility of a rural area.
   - Activities and Interests: Consider destinations that align with your hobbies, interests, and lifestyle preferences.

10. Infrastructure and Amenities
    - Accessibility: Look for destinations with good transportation links and infrastructure.
    - Amenities: Consider the availability of amenities such as grocery stores, gyms, and recreational facilities.

Examples of Digital Nomad-Friendly Destinations
- Bali, Indonesia: Affordable cost of living, vibrant digital nomad community, beautiful beaches, and tropical climate.
- Lisbon, Portugal: Affordable, good internet, rich culture, and historic architecture.
- Chiang Mai, Thailand: Low cost of living, reliable internet, vibrant expat community, and delicious food.
- Medellin, Colombia: Affordable, pleasant climate, modern amenities, and welcoming culture.
- Tallinn, Estonia: Highly digitalized, e-residency program, efficient public services, and a high quality of life.

Final Thoughts
When choosing your next destination as a digital nomad, consider your priorities, work requirements, budget, and personal preferences. Research thoroughly, connect with other digital nomads, and visit potential destinations before committing to a long-term stay. Flexibility is key, so be open to exploring new places and adapting to different environments to make the most of your digital nomad lifestyle.

Digital Nomad Lifestyle

2. Accommodation Options

Pros and cons of various living arrangements: co-living spaces, Airbnbs, hostels, and more. Choosing the right living arrangement is crucial for digital nomads, as it can impact your productivity, comfort, and overall experience. Here are the pros and cons of popular living arrangements:

1. Co-Living Spaces

Pros:

- Community: Opportunity to network and socialize with like-minded individuals.
- Convenience: Often include amenities like coworking spaces, cleaning services, and social events.
- Support: Access to staff for assistance with local information or issues.

Cons:

- Cost: Can be more expensive than other options, especially in popular digital nomad hubs.
- Noise: Limited privacy and potential for noise from other residents.
- Availability: Popular spaces may have limited availability, especially during peak seasons.

39

2. Airbnb

Pros:
- Flexibility: Choose from a variety of accommodations based on your preferences and budget.
- Comfort: Often more comfortable and private than other options
- Local Experience: Opportunity to stay in residential neighborhoods and experience local culture.

Cons:
- Cost: Can be more expensive, especially for short-term stays or in popular tourist destinations.
- Limited Services: May not have the same amenities or support as hotels or co-living spaces.
- Regulations: Some cities have strict regulations on short-term rentals, which could impact your stay.

3. Hostels

Pros:
- Affordability: Usually the most budget-friendly option, especially for solo travelers.
- Social Atmosphere: Opportunity to meet other travelers and participate in hostel activities.
- Services: Some hostels offer amenities like laundry facilities, common areas, and organized tours.

Cons:
- Privacy: Limited privacy, especially in dormitory-style accommodations.
- Noise: Can be noisy, especially if you're a light sleeper.
- Comfort: Basic amenities and shared facilities may not be suitable for long-term stays or remote work.

4. Hotels

Pros:
- Comfort: Generally offer higher levels of comfort and privacy.
- Services: Amenities like room service, housekeeping, and concierge services.
- Reliability: Consistent standards and quality of accommodation.

Cons:
- Cost: Typically more expensive than other options, especially for longer stays.
- Isolation: Less opportunity to socialize and connect with other travelers.
- Amenities: Limited kitchen facilities and common areas compared to co-living spaces or hostels.

Digital Nomad Lifestyle

5. Long-Term Rentals

Pros:
- Cost-Effective: Often cheaper than short-term stays, especially for extended periods.
- Local Experience: Opportunity to live like a local and immerse yourself in the culture.
- Comfort: More space and privacy compared to other options.

Cons:
- Commitment: Requires a longer commitment, which may not be suitable for all digital nomads.
- Furnishing: May need to purchase or rent furniture and household items.
- Responsibility: Responsible for utilities, maintenance, and other aspects of living.

Conclusion

The best living arrangement for you as a digital nomad depends on your budget, lifestyle preferences, and the nature of your work. Consider the pros and cons of each option, and choose the one that aligns with your priorities for a comfortable and productive experience while living and working remotely.

3. Staying Productive

Creating a productive work environment and managing time effectively

Maintaining a productive work environment and managing your time effectively are essential for digital nomads to balance work and travel. Here are some tips to help you stay focused and make the most of your time:

1. Designing Your Workspace
   - Ergonomic Setup: Invest in a comfortable chair and desk to avoid discomfort during long hours of work.
   - Good Lighting: Ensure your workspace is well-lit to reduce eye strain and improve focus.
   - Minimal Distractions: Choose a quiet area to work and minimize distractions such as noise and clutter.
   - Personalization: Personalize your workspace with items that inspire and motivate you.

2. Time Management Techniques
   - Prioritize Tasks: Use tools like Eisenhower Matrix or ABC prioritization to focus on important tasks
   - Pomodoro Technique: Work in intervals (e.g., 25 minutes of work followed by a 5-minute break) to maintain focus.

Digital Nomad Lifestyle

- Time Blocking: Allocate specific blocks of time for different tasks or types of work.
- Limit Multitasking: Focus on one task at a time to improve efficiency and reduce mental fatigue.

3. Setting Boundaries
   - Define Work Hours: Establish clear work hours to separate work from personal time.
   - Communicate Availability: Inform clients or colleagues of your availability and response times.
   - Learn to Say No: Prioritize your workload and decline tasks that do not align with your goals or schedule.

4. Managing Digital Distractions
   - Use Focus Apps: Use apps like Freedom, Stay Focused, or Cold Turkey to block distracting websites or apps.
   - Turn Off Notifications: Disable non-essential notifications on your devices to minimize interruptions.
   - Create a Digital Detox Routine: Designate specific times to check emails and social media to avoid constant distractions.

5. Health and Well-being
   - Regular Breaks: Take regular breaks to rest your eyes and stretch your body.
   - Stay Hydrated: Drink plenty of water throughout the day to stay hydrated and maintain focus.
   - Healthy Snacks: Keep healthy snacks on hand to maintain energy levels throughout the day.
   - Exercise: Incorporate physical activity into your routine to boost energy and improve focus.

6. Utilizing Technology and Tools
   - Task Management Apps: Use apps like Todoist, Trello, or Asana to organize tasks and track progress.
   - Calendar Apps: Use a calendar app to schedule tasks, meetings, and appointments.
   - Collaboration Tools: Use tools like Slack, Microsoft Teams, or Zoom for communication and collaboration with team members.

7. Reflect and Adjust
   - Regular Review: Review your progress and productivity regularly to identify areas for improvement.
   - Adjust Strategies: Be flexible and willing to adjust your strategies based on what works best for you.
   - Seek Feedback: Ask for feedback from colleagues, friends, or mentors to gain new insights and improve your productivity.

BharatVatsa

By implementing these tips and strategies, you can create a productive work environment and manage your time effectively as a digital nomad, allowing you to enjoy a successful and balanced lifestyle.

4. Building a Community

Connecting with other digital nomads and finding local communities.
Building connections with other digital nomads and local communities can enhance your travel experience and provide valuable support and insights. Here are some ways to connect with fellow nomads and find local communities:

1. Online Platforms and Forums
   - Digital Nomad Forums: Join online forums like Nomad List, Digital Nomad Forum, or Reddit's r/digitalnomad to connect with other nomads, ask questions, and share experiences.
   - Social Media Groups: Join Facebook groups, LinkedIn groups, or follow digital nomad accounts on Instagram for networking and community building.
   - Coworking Space Websites: Many coworking spaces have online communities where members can connect and collaborate.

2. Coworking Spaces and Meetup Groups
   - Coworking Spaces: Join coworking spaces in your destination city to meet other digital nomads and professionals.

- **Meetup.com:** Use Meetup to find local events, meetups, and networking opportunities for digital nomads and expats.
- **Local Expat Communities:** Attend expat gatherings or events to connect with other expats and learn about the local culture.

3. **Attend Digital Nomad Events and Conferences**
   - **Nomad Cruise:** Join a Nomad Cruise, a networking event where digital nomads travel together by cruise ship.
   - **Nomad Summit:** Attend the Nomad Summit, a conference for digital nomads to learn, network, and connect.
   - **Other Events:** Look for other digital nomad events and conferences happening in your area or online.

4. **Use Social Media and Networking Apps**
   - **LinkedIn:** Connect with other digital nomads, professionals, and potential clients on LinkedIn.
   - **Twitter:** Follow digital nomad hashtags and accounts to stay updated and engage with the community.
   - **Networking Apps:** Use apps like Shapr or Bumble Bizz to connect with professionals and expand your network.

5. **Join Remote Work and Travel Programs**
   - **Remote Year:** Join Remote Year, a program that facilitates travel and work experiences for digital nomads.
   - **Unsettled:** Participate in Unsettled retreats, which bring together a community of remote workers and creatives in different locations.

6. **Volunteer or Join Local Activities**
   - **Volunteer Opportunities:** Volunteer with local organizations or charities to meet locals and fellow travelers.
   - **Language Exchange:** Participate in language exchange programs or classes to meet locals and immerse yourself in the local culture.

7. **Create Your Own Meetups and Events**
   - **Host a Meetup:** Organize your own digital nomad meetup or event in your current location.
   - **Collaborate with Others:** Partner with local businesses or organizations to host joint events or workshops.

By actively seeking out and participating in these opportunities, you can connect with other digital nomads and local communities, enriching your travel experience and expanding your network.

5. Balancing Work & Leisure

Tips for maintaining work-life balance while exploring new places.
Maintaining work-life balance while exploring new places as a digital nomad is crucial for your well-being and productivity. Here are some tips to help you achieve a balance between work and leisure:

1. Establish a Routine
   - Set Work Hours: Establish a consistent work schedule to maintain a sense of routine.
   - Designate Workspace: Create a dedicated workspace to separate work from leisure.
   - Include Breaks: Schedule regular breaks to rest and recharge throughout the day.

2. Prioritize Tasks
   - Use Time Management Techniques: Prioritize tasks using methods like the Pomodoro Technique or Eisenhower Matrix.
   - Focus on Essential Tasks: Identify and focus on high-priority tasks to avoid feeling overwhelmed.
   - Delegate or Outsource: Delegate tasks or outsource work when possible to lighten your workload.

3. Stay Flexible
   - Embrace Flexibility: Embrace the flexibility of remote work to explore new places and experiences.

- Adapt to Changes: Be prepared for unexpected changes in your schedule or environment
- Adjust Your Routine: Modify your routine as needed to accommodate travel and new experiences.

4. Manage Your Energy
- Listen to Your Body: Pay attention to your energy levels and take breaks when needed.
- Maintain Healthy Habits: Eat well, exercise regularly, and get enough sleep to sustain your energy.
- Practice Mindfulness: Incorporate mindfulness practices such as meditation or yoga to reduce stress and stay present.

5. Set Boundaries
- Establish Boundaries: Set boundaries between work and leisure time to avoid overworking.
- Communicate Your Availability: Clearly communicate your work hours and availability to clients or colleagues.
- Learn to Say No: Prioritize your well-being by learning to say no to non-essential tasks or commitments.

6. Stay Connected
- Maintain Relationships: Stay connected with friends, family, and colleagues to nurture relationships.
- Network with Locals: Connect with locals and other travelers to build a sense of community.
- Join Social Activities: Participate in social activities and events to balance work with leisure.

7. Plan Your Travel Wisely
- Balance Work and Leisure: Plan your travel itinerary to include both work and leisure activities.
- Choose Accommodations Wisely: Select accommodations that offer a conducive environment for work and relaxation.
- Research Internet Connectivity: Ensure your accommodation and destinations have reliable internet access for work.

8. Reflect and Adjust
- Regular Reflection: Reflect on your work-life balance regularly and make adjustments as needed.
- Seek Feedback: Ask for feedback from colleagues, friends, or mentors to gain new perspectives.
- Be Open to Change: Be open to changing your approach to work and travel to achieve a better balance.

Digital Nomad Lifestyle

By incorporating these tips into your digital nomad lifestyle, you can maintain a healthy work-life balance while exploring new places and experiences.

PART:4 - CHALLENGES & SOLUTIONS

1. Dealing with Loneliness and Isolation

Strategies for combating loneliness and maintaining mental health

Loneliness and mental health can be significant challenges for digital nomads, especially when traveling solo or spending long periods away from home. Here are some strategies to help you combat loneliness and maintain your mental health:

1. Build a Support Network
    - Connect with Other Nomads: Join digital nomad communities, attend meetups, and use social media to connect with other travelers.
    - Stay in Touch: Regularly communicate with friends and family through calls, messages, or video chats.
    - Seek Professional Help: Consider online therapy or counseling services if you're feeling overwhelmed or isolated.

2. Establish a Routine
    - Set Regular Work Hours: Establish a consistent work schedule to provide structure and stability.

- **Include Self-Care Activities:** Incorporate activities you enjoy, such as exercise, hobbies, or meditation, into your daily routine.
- **Plan Social Interactions:** Schedule social activities or outings to break up your routine and prevent isolation.

3. **Engage in Social Activities**
   - **Attend Local Events:** Participate in local events, festivals, or classes to meet new people and experience the local culture.
   - **Join Social Groups:** Join clubs, classes, or sports teams to meet like-minded individuals and build friendships.
   - **Volunteer:** Volunteer with local organizations to connect with the community and make a positive impact.

4. **Stay Active and Healthy**
   - **Exercise Regularly:** Engage in physical activity to boost your mood and energy levels.
   - **Eat Well:** Maintain a balanced diet to support your physical and mental health.
   - **Get Enough Sleep:** Prioritize sleep to improve your mood, cognitive function, and overall well-being.

5. **Practice Mindfulness and Relaxation Techniques**
   - **Mindfulness Meditation:** Practice mindfulness meditation to reduce stress and increase self-awareness.
   - **Deep Breathing Exercises:** Use deep breathing techniques to calm your mind and body in stressful situations.
   - **Yoga or Tai Chi:** Engage in yoga or tai chi to improve your mental and physical well-being.

6. **Stay Engaged with Your Work**
   - **Set Goals:** Establish clear goals for your work to stay motivated and focused.
   - **Stay Inspired:** Seek out new challenges and learning opportunities to stay engaged with your work.
   - **Collaborate with Others:** Collaborate with colleagues or fellow nomads to stay connected and inspired.

7. **Embrace the Digital Nomad Lifestyle**
   - **Focus on the Positives:** Embrace the freedom, adventure, and personal growth that come with the digital nomad lifestyle.
   - **Stay Flexible:** Be open to new experiences and changes in your plans to adapt to the nomadic lifestyle.
   - **Seek Balance:** Strive for a balance between work, travel, and personal time to avoid burnout and maintain well-being.

8. Monitor Your Mental Health
- **Stay Mindful of Your Feelings:** Pay attention to your emotions and seek help if you're feeling overwhelmed or depressed.
- **Seek Professional Help:** Reach out to mental health professionals or counselors if you need support or guidance.
- **Stay Informed:** Learn about mental health resources and services available in your location or online.

By implementing these strategies, you can combat loneliness, maintain your mental health, and enjoy a fulfilling digital nomad lifestyle.

2. Overcoming Burnout

Recognizing and preventing burnout in a constantly changing environment.
Burnout is a real risk for digital nomads due to the constant change and lack of routine. Here are some strategies to help you recognize and prevent burnout:

1. Recognizing Burnout
    - Physical Symptoms: Pay attention to physical signs such as fatigue, headaches, or changes in appetite.
    - Emotional Exhaustion: Feeling drained, overwhelmed, or emotionally detached from work.
    - Cynicism and Detachment: Negative or cynical feelings towards work, clients, or colleagues.
    - Reduced Performance: Decreased productivity, difficulty concentrating, or making errors.
    - Lack of Satisfaction: Loss of enjoyment in work or feeling unfulfilled despite accomplishments

2. Preventing Burnout
    - Set Boundaries: Establish clear boundaries between work and personal time.
    - Maintain a Routine: Create a flexible routine that includes regular work hours, breaks, and time for relaxation.

Digital Nomad Lifestyle

- Practice Self-Care: Prioritize activities that promote physical and mental well-being, such as exercise, healthy eating, and sufficient sleep.
- Seek Social Support: Stay connected with friends, family, and other digital nomads for emotional support.
- Manage Workload: Prioritize tasks, delegate when possible, and set realistic goals to avoid feeling overwhelmed.
- Take Regular Breaks: Incorporate short breaks throughout your workday to rest and recharge.
- Engage in Mindfulness: Practice mindfulness techniques such as meditation or deep breathing to reduce stress.
- Stay Flexible: Embrace change and uncertainty as part of the digital nomad lifestyle, but also know when to say no to avoid overcommitting.
- Seek Professional Help: If you're experiencing persistent feelings of burnout, consider seeking help from a mental health professional.

3. Coping with Burnout
- Take Time Off: If possible, take a break from work to rest and rejuvenate.
- Reevaluate Your Goals: Reflect on your priorities and make adjustments to align with your values and interests.
- Seek Feedback: Talk to trusted colleagues, friends, or mentors for feedback and support.
- Explore New Opportunities: Consider exploring new projects, hobbies, or locations to reignite your passion and motivation.
- Practice Gratitude: Focus on the positive aspects of your life and work to cultivate a sense of gratitude.
- Learn from Experience: Use your experience of burnout as an opportunity for growth and self-improvement.

By being aware of the signs of burnout and taking proactive steps to prevent it, you can maintain a healthy work-life balance and continue to thrive as a digital nomad.

3. Staying Safe on the Road

Personal safety tips and navigating unfamiliar territories
Exploring new places as a digital nomad can be exciting, but it's important to prioritize your safety. Here are some tips to help you stay safe while navigating unfamiliar territories:

1. Research Your Destination
    - Learn About the Culture: Familiarize yourself with the local customs, traditions, and cultural norms to avoid misunderstandings.
    - Understand the Laws: Research the local laws and regulations, especially regarding safety, health, and travel.
    - Know the Emergency Numbers: Memorize or keep a list of emergency numbers for the local police, ambulance, and embassy.

2. Stay Aware of Your Surroundings
    - Stay Vigilant: Be aware of your surroundings and avoid risky areas, especially at night.

- **Trust Your Instincts:** If something feels wrong or unsafe, trust your instincts and leave the area.
- **Avoid Displaying Valuables:** Keep your valuables, such as phones, cameras, and laptops, out of sight to avoid attracting attention.

3. Secure Your Belongings
   - **Use Anti-Theft Gear:** Invest in anti-theft backpacks, bags, or locks to secure your belongings.
   - **Backup Important Documents:** Keep copies of your passport, ID, and other important documents in a secure location or digitally.

4. Stay Connected
   - **Share Your Itinerary:** Inform someone you trust about your travel plans, including your destination and expected return date.
   - **Use GPS and Maps:** Use GPS apps or maps to navigate unfamiliar areas and avoid getting lost.

5. Use Safe Transportation
   - **Choose Reliable Transport:** Use reputable transportation services, such as taxis or ride-sharing apps, especially at night.
   - **Avoid Hitchhiking:** Avoid hitchhiking or accepting rides from strangers to reduce the risk of danger.

6. Be Mindful of Scams and Fraud
   - **Stay Alert for Scams:** Be cautious of scams targeting tourists and avoid offers that seem too good to be true.
   - **Use Secure Payment Methods:** Use secure payment methods and be wary of sharing financial information in unfamiliar places.

7. Respect Local Customs and Traditions
   - **Dress Appropriately:** Dress modestly and respect local dress codes, especially in conservative areas.
   - **Be Respectful:** Respect local customs, traditions, and beliefs to avoid unintentional offense.

8. Stay Healthy and Hydrated
   - **Drink Safe Water:** Drink bottled or filtered water to avoid waterborne illnesses.
   - **Practice Food Safety:** Eat at reputable restaurants and be cautious of street food to prevent food poisoning.

9. Learn Basic Phrases
   - Learn Local Phrases: Learn basic phrases in the local language, such as greetings and asking for help, to communicate effectively.

10. Stay Informed
    - Stay Updated: Stay informed about local news, weather, and safety alerts to avoid potential risks.
    - Seek Local Advice: Ask locals or other travelers for advice on staying safe in the area.

By following these tips and staying vigilant, you can enhance your safety while exploring new places as a digital nomad.

PART:5 - ADVANCED NOMAD STRATEGIES

1. Scaling Your Remote Business

Growing your freelance business or remote job into a sustainable career
Transitioning from a freelance or remote job into a sustainable career requires strategic planning, consistent effort, and a focus on long-term growth. Here are some key steps to help you build a successful and sustainable career:

1. Define Your Goals and Vision
   - **Set Clear Goals:** Define your long-term career goals and create a roadmap to achieve them.
   - **Identify Your Niche:** Determine your niche or specialization to stand out in the market and attract clients or employers.
   - **Develop Your Brand:** Build a strong personal brand that reflects your expertise, values, and unique selling points.

2. Build a Strong Online Presence
   - **Professional Website:** Create a professional website that showcases your portfolio, services, and testimonials.
   - **Optimize Your LinkedIn Profile:** Use LinkedIn to network, showcase your skills, and connect with potential clients or employers.
   - **Utilize Social Media:** Use social media platforms to promote your work, engage with your audience, and build your brand.

3. Expand Your Network

- **Attend Networking Events:** Attend industry events, conferences, and meetups to expand your network and build relationships.
- **Join Online Communities:** Join online forums, groups, and communities relevant to your industry to connect with peers and potential clients.
- **Collaborate with Others:** Collaborate with other freelancers, professionals, or businesses to expand your reach and opportunities.

4. Enhance Your Skills and Expertise

- **Continuous Learning:** Stay updated with industry trends and developments through online courses, workshops, and certifications.
- **Seek Feedback:** Request feedback from clients, colleagues, or mentors to improve your skills and performance.
- **Specialize and Diversify:** Consider specializing in a niche area or diversifying your services to attract a wider range of clients or employers.

5. Provide Excellent Service and Value

- **Client Relationships:** Build strong relationships with your clients by delivering high-quality work and exceeding expectations.
- **Value Proposition:** Clearly communicate the value you provide to clients or employers and how you can help solve their problems.
- **Feedback Loop:** Encourage feedback from clients to understand their needs better and improve your services.

6. Manage Your Finances and Plan for the Future

- **Financial Planning:** Manage your finances effectively, including budgeting, saving, and investing for the future.
- **Create a Business Plan:** Develop a business plan that outlines your goals, strategies, and financial projections for growth.

- **Diversify Income Streams:** Explore opportunities to diversify your income streams, such as passive income or multiple clients/employers.

7. Adapt to Change and Stay Flexible
- **Embrace Change:** Stay adaptable and open to new opportunities, technologies, and ways of working.
- **Stay Updated:** Keep abreast of industry trends, market demands, and changes in your field to remain competitive.
- **Seek Feedback:** Regularly assess your progress, seek feedback from clients or peers, and make adjustments as needed.

By following these steps and staying committed to your growth, you can turn your freelance business or remote job into a sustainable and successful career.

2. Passive Income Streams

Exploring passive income opportunities to support your nomadic lifestyle

Exploring passive income opportunities can provide a valuable source of income while you focus on your digital nomad lifestyle. Here are some passive income ideas to consider:

1. **Create and Sell Digital Products:** Develop and sell digital products such as e-books, online courses, stock photos, or digital artwork.
2. **Affiliate Marketing:** Promote products or services and earn a commission for each sale or referral made through your affiliate link.
3. **Drop shipping:** Start an e-commerce store without holding inventory by partnering with suppliers who ship products directly to customers.
4. **Print on Demand:** Design and sell custom-printed products like t-shirts, mugs, or phone cases without managing inventory or shipping.
5. **Invest in Stocks or Dividend-Paying Funds:** Invest in stocks or dividend-paying funds to earn passive income through dividends and capital gains.

6. **Real Estate Crowdfunding:** Invest in real estate projects through crowdfunding platforms to earn rental income or capital appreciation.
7. **Peer-to-Peer Lending:** Lend money to individuals or businesses through peer-to-peer lending platforms and earn interest on your investment.
8. **Create a YouTube Channel or Podcast:** Create content on a topic you're passionate about and monetize it through ads, sponsorships, or merchandise sales.
9. **Create a Membership Site:** Offer premium content, courses, or services to members who pay a subscription fee.
10. **License Your Photos, Videos, or Music:** Sell the rights to your creative work to individuals or businesses for use in their projects.

It's important to research and choose passive income streams that align with your skills, interests, and financial goals. Diversifying your passive income sources can also help mitigate risk and create a more stable income stream.

3. Continuous Learning and Skill Development

Staying competitive and constantly upgrading your skills

Staying competitive and continuously upgrading your skills is essential in today's rapidly evolving job market, especially as a digital nomad. Here are some strategies to help you stay ahead:

1. Lifelong Learning
   - Online Courses: Enroll in online courses on platforms like Coursera, Udemy, or LinkedIn Learning to learn new skills or deepen existing ones.
   - Webinars and Workshops: Attend webinars and workshops to stay updated on industry trends and best practices.
   - Certifications: Obtain relevant certifications to demonstrate your expertise and commitment to professional development.

2. Networking and Collaboration
   - Join Professional Networks: Join industry-specific groups, forums, or associations to network with peers and stay informed.

- **Collaborate with Others:** Collaborate on projects or initiatives with other professionals to gain new perspectives and skills.
- **Mentorship:** Seek mentorship from experienced professionals in your field to guide your career growth.

3. **Skill Diversification**
   - **Cross-Training:** Learn complementary skills or explore new areas related to your field to broaden your expertise.
   - **Soft Skills Development:** Develop soft skills such as communication, leadership, and adaptability to enhance your professional profile.

4. **Stay Updated with Industry Trends**
   - **Read Industry Publications:** Stay informed by reading industry publications, blogs, and news articles.
   - **Attend Conferences and Events:** Participate in industry conferences and events to learn about the latest trends and innovations.
   - **Follow Thought Leaders:** Follow thought leaders and influencers in your field on social media to stay updated on industry developments.

5. **Adaptability and Flexibility**
   - **Embrace Change:** Be open to new technologies, trends, and ways of working to adapt to changing market demands.
   - **Upskill for Future Roles:** Anticipate future skill requirements and proactively upskill to meet the demands of future roles.

6. **Feedback and Self-Reflection**
   - **Seek Feedback:** Request feedback from colleagues, clients, or mentors to identify areas for improvement.
   - **Self-Reflection:** Reflect on your experiences and challenges to learn from them and improve your skills.

7. **Time Management and Focus**
   - **Prioritize Learning:** Allocate dedicated time for learning and skill development in your schedule.
   - **Focus on High-Impact Skills:** Identify and focus on skills that will have the greatest impact on your career and goals.

By implementing these strategies, you can stay competitive, continuously improve your skills, and remain relevant in the ever-changing digital landscape as a digital nomad.

CONCLUSION

1. The Future of Digital Nomadism

Trends and predictions for the future of remote work and the digital nomad movement

The future of remote work and the digital nomad movement is expected to be influenced by several key trends and predictions:

1. Increased Remote Work Opportunities
   - Hybrid Work Models: Companies are likely to adopt hybrid work models, allowing employees to work both remotely and in the office.
   - Global Talent Pool: Organizations will tap into a global talent pool, hiring remote workers from around the world.
   - Freelance Economy: The freelance economy will continue to grow, offering more opportunities for remote work and independent contractors.

2. Technological Advancements
- Virtual Reality (VR) and Augmented Reality (AR): VR and AR technologies will enhance remote collaboration and communication.
- Artificial Intelligence (AI) and Automation: AI and automation will streamline processes and tasks, making remote work more efficient.
- Internet Connectivity: Improved internet connectivity in remote areas will enable more people to work from anywhere.

3. Focus on Well-being and Work-Life Balance
- Flexible Schedules: More emphasis will be placed on flexible work schedules to accommodate individual preferences and lifestyles.
- Mental Health Support: Employers will offer more mental health support and resources for remote workers.
- Work-Life Integration: The boundary between work and personal life will continue to blur, with a focus on work-life integration rather than separation.

4. Sustainable and Eco-Friendly Practices
- Reduced Carbon Footprint: Remote work will contribute to reducing carbon emissions from commuting and office-related activities.
- Digital Nomadism: The digital nomad lifestyle will evolve to incorporate more sustainable practices, such as eco-friendly accommodations and transportation.

5. Legal and Regulatory Changes
- Remote Work Policies: Governments and organizations will establish clearer policies and regulations for remote work.
- Visa and Immigration Policies: Countries will introduce new visa and immigration policies to attract remote workers and digital nomads.

6. Evolution of Workspaces
- Remote Workspaces: More companies will invest in creating remote workspaces or coworking spaces for their employees.
- Home Office Design: There will be a focus on designing home offices for comfort, productivity, and ergonomics.

7. Rise of Digital Nomad Hubs
- Digital Nomad Communities: The number of digital nomad communities and hubs around the world will continue to grow.
- Infrastructure Development: Countries and cities will invest in infrastructure to attract and support digital nomads, such as high-speed internet and coworking spaces.

Overall, the future of remote work and the digital nomad movement looks promising, with opportunities for growth, innovation, and a more flexible and inclusive work environment.

2. Final Thoughts and Inspiration

Encouragement and motivation for readers embarking on their digital nomad journey

Embarking on a digital nomad journey is an exciting and life-changing decision. It's a path filled with adventure, learning, and personal growth. Here's some encouragement and motivation for those starting their digital nomad journey:

1. Embrace the Unknown: The unknown can be daunting, but it's also where you'll find the most growth and discovery. Embrace the adventure of exploring new places and cultures.
2. Focus on Personal Growth: The digital nomad lifestyle offers unique opportunities for personal growth. Embrace challenges as opportunities to learn and develop new skills.

3. **Build Resilience:** The digital nomad lifestyle can be unpredictable. Build resilience and adaptability to navigate challenges and setbacks.
4. **Create Your Own Path:** As a digital nomad, you have the freedom to create your own path. Take the time to define what success means to you and pursue it wholeheartedly.
5. **Stay Connected:** While the digital nomad lifestyle can be solitary at times, it's important to stay connected with others. Build a strong support network of friends, family, and fellow nomads.
6. **Celebrate Small Wins:** Celebrate your achievements, no matter how small. Each step forward is a step closer to your goals.
7. **Practice Gratitude:** Gratitude can transform any journey. Take time to appreciate the experiences, people, and opportunities that come your way.
8. **Stay Curious:** The world is full of wonders. Stay curious and open-minded, and you'll discover new perspectives and possibilities.
9. **Stay Flexible:** The digital nomad lifestyle is all about flexibility. Embrace change and be open to new opportunities that come your way.
10. **Believe in Yourself:** You have the courage and the ability to create the life you want. Believe in yourself and your dreams.

Remember, the digital nomad lifestyle is a journey, not a destination. Enjoy the ride, stay true to yourself, and embrace the adventure ahead!

APPENDICES

1. Resources and References

Useful links, websites, and books for further reading

Websites and Blogs
1. Nomad List: https://nomadlist.com/ - A comprehensive resource for digital nomads, including city rankings, cost of living, and community discussions.
2. Remote OK: https://remoteok.com/ - A job board featuring remote job opportunities across various industries.
3. Digital Nomad World: https://digitalnomads.world/ - A platform offering resources, guides, and community support for digital nomads.
4. The Remote Life: https://www.theremotelife.com/ - A blog with tips, guides, and stories about living and working remotely.
5. Reddit: https://www.reddit.com/r/digitalnomad - A Reddit community where digital nomads share experiences, advice, and resources.
6. Nomadic Matt: https://www.nomadicmatt.com/ - Travel blog with tips on budget travel, working remotely, and living as a digital nomad.

Digital Nomad Lifestyle

Books
1. "The 4-Hour Workweek" by Timothy Ferriss - A seminal book that explores the possibilities of remote work and lifestyle design.
2. "Digital Nomads: How to Live, Work and Play Around the World" by Esther Jacobs and André Gussekloo - A practical guide for those looking to embrace the digital nomad lifestyle.
3. "Remote: Office Not Required" by Jason Fried and David Heinemeier Hansson - A book that discusses the benefits and challenges of remote work.
4. "The Digital Nomad Handbook" by Lonely Planet - A comprehensive guide with practical advice and insights for digital nomads.
5. "How to Travel the World on $50 a Day" by Matt Kepnes - A book focused on budget travel, including tips for digital nomads.
6. "Nomad Capitalist: How to Reclaim Your Freedom with Offshore Companies, Dual Citizenship, Foreign Banks, and Overseas Investments" by Andrew Henderson - A guide on international living and financial strategies for digital nomads.

Tools and Resources
1. Trello: https://trello.com/ - A project management tool to organize tasks and collaborate with team members.
2. Slack: https://slack.com/intl/en-in/ - A communication platform for remote teams.
3. Zoom: https://zoom.us/ - A video conferencing tool for virtual meetings.
4. Microsoft OneNote: https://www.onenote.com/ - A note-taking app to keep your ideas and plans organized.
5. Google Workspace: https://workspace.google.com/ - A suite of productivity and collaboration tools.
6. Wise: https://wise.com/ - A money transfer service for managing international payments with low fees.

Online Learning Platforms
1. Coursera: https://www.coursera.org/en-IN - Offers online courses from universities and companies to help you upgrade your skills.
2. Udemy: https://www.udemy.com/ - A platform with a wide range of courses on various topics, including freelancing and remote work.
3. LinkedIn Learning: https://www.linkedin.com/learning/ - Provides courses on professional development and skill-building.

By exploring these resources, you can gain valuable insights, tools, and strategies to support your digital nomad journey and ensure a successful and fulfilling lifestyle.

2. Templates and Checklists

Packing lists, budget templates, and other practical tools

Packing Lists
Basic Packing List for Digital Nomads

1. Electronics: Laptop and charger, Smartphone and charger, Portable hard drive or SSD, Power bank, Universal adapter, Noise-canceling headphones, USB flash drives, Travel router, External keyboard and mouse (optional)
2. Clothing: Lightweight, versatile clothing, Comfortable shoes, Weather-appropriate outerwear, Swimwear, Sleepwear, Undergarments and socks, Workout clothes
3. Toiletries: Travel-sized toiletries (shampoo, conditioner, soap) Toothbrush and toothpaste, Razor and shaving cream, Deodorant, Skincare products, Prescription medications, First aid kit

Digital Nomad Lifestyle

4. **Travel Essentials:** Passport and copies, Travel insurance documents, Vaccination records (if necessary) Credit and debit cards, Emergency cash, Travel pillow and eye mask, Reusable water bottle, Travel towel
5. **Miscellaneous:** Backpack or daypack, Packing cubes, Ziplock bags, Journal and pens, Books or e-reader, Sunglasses and hat

Minimalist Packing List
1. Electronics: Laptop and charger, Smartphone and charger, Power bank, Universal adapter
2. Clothing: 2-3 versatile outfits 1 pair of comfortable shoes, Weather-appropriate outerwear, Minimal undergarments and socks
3. Toiletries: Essential travel-sized toiletries, Toothbrush and toothpaste, Deodorant, Prescription medications
4. Travel Essentials: Passport and copies, Travel insurance documents, Credit and debit cards, Emergency cash
5. Miscellaneous: Small backpack, Packing cubes (optional) Reusable water bottle

Budget Templates: (feel free to modify as needed)

1. Basic Monthly Budget Template

CATEGORY	BUDGETED AMOUNT	ACTUAL AMOUNT
INCOME		
Salary		
Freelance Income		
Passive Income		
Other Income		
EXPENSES		
Housing		
Utilities		
Internet/Phone		
Transportation		
Groceries		
Dining Out		
Health Insurance		
Travel Insurance		
Entertainment		
Fitness/Wellness		
Subscriptions		
Savings/Investments		
Miscellaneous		
Total Expenses		
Net Income		

2. Travel Expense Tracker Template

Date	Description	Category	Amount	Currency	Notes
MM-DD-YYYY	Accommodation	Housing			
MM-DD-YYYY	Flight Ticket	Transportation			
MM-DD-YYYY	Restaurant Meal	Dining Out			
MM-DD-YYYY	Museum Ticket	Entertainment			
MM-DD-YYYY	SIM Card	Communication			
MM-DD-YYYY	Gym Pass	Fitness			
MM-DD-YYYY	Grocery Shopping	Groceries			

Other Practical Tools

1. Trello: Organize tasks and projects using boards and cards.
2. Google Sheets: Create and manage budget templates and travel expense trackers.
3. Notion: All-in-one workspace for notes, tasks, and projects.
4. TripIt: Plan and organize travel itineraries.
5. Wise (formerly TransferWise): Manage international payments and transfers.
6. Trail Wallet (or any other): Expense tracker app designed for travelers.
7. Slack/Zoom/Teams: Communication tool for remote teams and communities.
8. Microsoft OneNote: Note-taking app for organizing thoughts, ideas, and documents.
9. Google Drive: Cloud storage for accessing important documents and files anywhere.

These practical tools and resources will help you stay organized, manage your finances, and ensure a smooth and enjoyable digital nomad experience.

www.ingramcontent.com/pod-product-compliance
Lightning Source LLC
Chambersburg PA
CBHW071951210526
45479CB00003B/900